Oscar Wilde

Selected by
Robert Mighall

D1644550

PHOENIX

This edition first published in 2010
Phoenix edition first published in 2003

Selection © J. M. Dent 1996
Chronology and glossary © J. M. Dent 2003

Typeset by Deltatype Ltd, Birkenhead, Merseyside
Printed in Great Britain by Clays Ltd, St Ives plc

A CIP catalogue reference for this book
is available from the British Library.

The Orion Publishing Group
Orion House
5 Upper St Martin's Lane
London
WC2H 9EA

Contents

Note on the Text

This volume contains a few poems which are taken
from 'manuscript' sources, including 'O Golden Queen
of life and joy', 'Desespoir', 'Pan: Double Villanelle'
and 'La Circassienne'. These are taken from
transcriptions of manuscripts which remained
unpublished during Wilde's lifetime. These copies were
made in 1908 by Walter Ledger, friend of Robert Ross
and Stuart Mason who were working on the Collected
Edition of Wilde's works at this time. They are found
in the Robert Ross Memorial Collection held by the
Bodleian Library, Oxford (Ross. MS. 9).

Oscar Wilde

Hélas!

To drift with every passion till my soul
Is a stringed lute on which all winds can play,
Is it for this that I have given away
Mine ancient wisdom, and austere control?
Methinks my life is a twice-written scroll
Scrawled over on some boyish holiday
With idle songs for pipe and virelay,
Which do but mar the secret of the whole.
Surely there was a time I might have trod
The sunlit heights, and from life's dissonance
Struck one clear chord to reach the ears of God:
Is that time dead? lo! with a little rod
I did but touch the honey of romance—
And must I lose a soul's inheritance?

Sonnet to Liberty

Not that I love thy children, whose dull eyes
See nothing save their own unlovely woe,
Whose minds know nothing, nothing care to know,—
But that the roar of thy Democracies,
Thy reigns of Terror, thy great Anarchies,
Mirror my wildest passions like the sea
And give my rage a brother – ! Liberty!
For this sake only do thy dissonant cries
Delight my discreet soul, else might all kings
By bloody knout or treacherous cannonades
Rob nations of their rights inviolate
And I remain unmoved – and yet, and yet,
These Christs that die upon the barricades,
God knows it I am with them, in some things.

Theoretikos

This mighty empire hath but feet of clay:
  Of all its ancient chivalry and might
  Our little island is forsaken quite:
Some enemy hath stolen its crown of bay,
And from its hills that voice hath passed away
  Which spake of Freedom: O come out of it,
  Come out of it, my Soul, thou art not fit
For this vile traffic-house, where day by day
  Wisdom and reverence are sold at mart,
  And the rude people rage with ignorant cries
Against an heritage of centuries.
  It mars my calm: wherefore in dreams of Art
  And loftiest culture I would stand apart,
Neither for God, nor for his enemies.

Requiescat

Tread lightly, she is near
  Under the snow,
Speak gently, she can hear
  The daisies grow.

All her bright golden hair
  Tarnished with rust,
She that was young and fair
  Fallen to dust.

Lily-like, white as snow,
  She hardly knew
She was a woman, so
  Sweetly she grew.

Coffin-board, heavy stone,
  Lie on her breast,
I vex my heart alone,
  She is at rest.

Peace, Peace, she cannot hear
  Lyre or sonnet,
All my life's buried here,
  Heap earth upon it.

San Miniato

See, I have climbed the mountain side
Up to this holy house of God,
Where once that Angel-Painter trod
Who saw the heavens opened wide,

And throned upon the crescent moon
The Virginal white Queen of Grace,—
Mary! could I but see thy face
Death could not come at all too soon.

O crowned by God with thorns and pain!
Mother of Christ! O mystic wife!
My heart is weary of this life
And over-sad to sing again.

O crowned by God with love and flame!
O crowned by Christ the Holy One!
O listen ere the searching sun
Show to the world my sin and shame.

Sonnet
On hearing the Dies Iræ sung in the Sistine Chapel

Nay, Lord, not thus! white lilies in the spring,
  Sad olive-groves, or silver-breasted dove,
  Teach me more clearly of Thy life and love
Than terrors of red flame and thundering.
The hillside vines dear memories of Thee bring:
  A bird at evening flying to its nest
  Tells me of One who had no place of rest:
I think it is of Thee the sparrows sing.
Come rather on some autumn afternoon,
  When red and brown are burnished on the leaves,
  And the fields echo to the gleaner's song,
Come when the splendid fulness of the moon
  Looks down upon the rows of golden sheaves,
  And reap Thy harvest: we have waited long.

Ave Maria Plena Gratia

Was this His coming! I had hoped to see
  A scene of wondrous glory, as was told
  Of some great God who in a rain of gold
Broke open bars and fell on Danae:
Or a dread vision as when Semele
  Sickening for love and unappeased desire
  Prayed to see God's clear body, and the fire
Caught her brown limbs and slew her utterly:
With such glad dreams I sought this holy place,
  And now with wondering eyes and heart I stand
  Before this supreme mystery of Love:
Some kneeling girl with passionless pale face,
  An angel with a lily in his hand,
  And over both the white wings of a Dove.

Madonna Mia

A lily-girl, not made for this world's pain,
  With brown, soft hair close braided by her ears,
  And longing eyes half veiled by slumberous tears
Like bluest water seen through mists of rain:
Pale cheeks whereon no love hath left its stain,
  Red underlip drawn in for fear of love,
  And white throat, whiter than the silvered dove,
Through whose wan marble creeps one purple vein.
Yet, though my lips shall praise her without cease,
  Even to kiss her feet I am not bold,
  Being o'ershadowed by the wings of awe.
Like Dante, when he stood with Beatrice
  Beneath the flaming Lion's breast, and saw
  The seventh Crystal, and the Stair of Gold.

Untitled

O Golden Queen of life and joy!
  O Lily without blot or stain!
O Loved as only loves a boy!
  O Loved in vain! O Loved in vain!

Ah, what to thee is war or peace,
  Who holdest all the keys of life,
Though the white fleets of gold should cease,
  And the blue seas be vexed with strife!

Bring poppy flower and poppy root,
  And yellow-petaled mandragore,
Bring berries of that purple fruit
  Which sleeps on Ocean's sleepless shore.

And when remorse and ruin come,
  And the glad pulse of youth is low,
O Helen! Helen! mingle some
  Divine nepenthe for my woe.

Till o'er the flower-foamed fields of sea
  On violet wing night steals away,
And God's white fingers open wide
  The crimson lips of risen day.

Tristitiæ

O well for him who lives at ease
 With garned gold in wide domain!
 Nor heeds the splashing of the rain,
The crashing down of forest trees.

O well for him who ne'er hath known
 The travail of the hungry years,
 A father grey with grief and tears,
A mother weeping all alone.

But well for him whose feet have trod
 The weary road of earthly strife,
 Yet from the sorrows of his life
Builds ladders to be nearer God.

Desespoir

The seasons mend their ruin as they go,
For in the spring the narciss shows its head
Nor withers till the rose has flamed to red,
And in the autumn purple violets blow,
And the slim crocus stirs the winter snow;
Wherefore yon leafless trees will bloom again
And this grey land grow green with summer rain
And send up cowslips for some boy to mow.
But what of life whose bitter hungry sea
Flows at our heels, and gloom of sunless night
Covers the days which never more return?
Ambition, love and all the thoughts that burn
We lose too soon, and only find delight
In withered husks of some dead memory.

The Grave of Keats

Rid of the world's injustice, and his pain,
  He rests at last beneath God's veil of blue:
  Taken from life when life and love were new
The youngest of the martyrs here is lain,
Fair as Sebastian, and as early slain.
  No cypress shades his grave or funeral yew,
  But gentle violets weeping with the dew
Weave on his bones an everblossoming chain.
O proudest heart that broke for misery!
  O sweetest lips since those of Mitylene!
  O poet-painter of our English Land!
Thy name was writ in water — it shall stand:
  And tears like mine shall keep thy memory green,
  As Isabella did her Basil-Tree.

Magdalen Walks

The little white clouds are racing over the sky,
  And the fields are strewn with the gold of the flower
    of March,
  The daffodil breaks under foot, and the tasselled larch
Sways and swings as the thrush goes hurrying by.

A delicate odour is borne on the wings of the morning
    breeze,
  The odour of deep wet grass, and of brown new-
    furrowed earth,
  The birds are singing for joy of the Spring's glad
    birth,
Hopping from branch to branch on the rocking trees.

And all the woods are alive with the murmur and
    sound of Spring,
  And the rosebud breaks into pink on the climbing
    briar,
  And the crocus-bed is a quivering moon of fire
Girdled round with the belt of an amethyst ring.

And the plane to the pine-tree is whispering some tale
    of love
  Till it rustles with laughter and tosses its mantle of
    green,
  And the gloom of the wych-elm's hollow is lit with
    the iris sheen
Of the burnished rainbow throat and the silver breast
    of a dove.

See! the lark starts up from his bed in the meadow
    there,

Breaking the gossamer threads and the nets of dew,
And flashing a-down the river, a flame of blue!
The kingfisher flies like an arrow, and wounds the air.

Chanson

A ring of gold and a milk-white dove
  Are goodly gifts for thee,
And a hempen rope for your own love
  To hang upon a tree.

For you a House of Ivory
  (Roses are white in the rose-bower)!
A narrow bed for me to lie
  (White, O white, is the hemlock flower)!

Myrtle and jessamine for you
  (O the red rose is fair to see)!
For me the cypress and the rue
  (Fairest of all is rose-mary)!

For you three lovers of your hand
  (Green grass where a man lies dead)!
For me three paces on the sand
  (Plant lilies at my head)!

Pan: Double Villanelle

I

O GOAT-FOOT GOD of Arcady!
  This modern world is grey and old,
And what remains to us of thee?

No more the shepherd lads in glee
  Throw apples at thy wattled fold.
O goat-foot God of Arcady!

Nor through the laurels can one see
  Thy soft brown limbs, thy beard of gold,
And what remains to us of thee?

And dull and dead our Thames would be
  For here the winds are chill and cold,
O goat-foot God of Arcady!

Then keep the tomb of Helicé,
  Thine olive-woods, thy vine-clad wold,
And what remains to us of thee?

Though many an unsung elegy
  Sleeps in the reeds our rivers hold,
O goat-foot God of Arcady!
Ah, what remains to us of thee?

II

AH, leave the hills of Arcady,
  Thy satyrs and their wanton play,
This modern world hath need of thee.

No nymph or Faun indeed have we,
  For Faun and nymph are old and grey,
Ah, leave the hills of Arcady!

This is the land where Liberty
  Lit grave-browed Milton on his way,
This modern world hath need of thee!

A land of ancient chivalry
  Where gentle Sidney saw the day,
Ah, leave the hills of Arcady!

This fierce sea-lion of the sea,
  This England, lacks some stronger lay,
This modern world hath need of thee!

Then blow some trumpet loud and free,
  And give thine oaten pipe away,
Ah, leave the hills of Arcady!
This modern world hath need of thee!

from The Garden of Eros

It is full summer now, the heart of June,
  Not yet the sun-burnt reapers are a-stir
Upon the upland meadow where too soon
  Rich autumn time, the season's usurer,
Will lend his hoarded gold to all the trees,
And see his treasure scattered by the wild and spend-
    thrift breeze.

Too soon indeed! yet here the daffodil,
  That love-child of the Spring, has lingered on
To vex the rose with jealousy, and still
  The harebell spreads her azure pavilion,
And like a strayed and wandering reveller
Abandoned of its brothers, whom long since June's
    messenger

The missel-thrush has frighted from the glade,
  One pale narcissus loiters fearfully
Close to a shadowy nook, where half afraid
  Of their own loveliness some violets lie
That will not look the gold sun in the face
For fear of too much splendour, – ah! methinks it is a
    place

Which should be trodden by Persephone
  When wearied of the flowerless fields of Dis!
Or danced on by the lads of Arcady!
  The hidden secret of eternal bliss
Known to the Grecian here a man might find,
Ah! you and I may find it now if Love and Sleep be
    kind.

* * *

Spirit of Beauty! tarry still a-while,
  They are not dead, thine ancient votaries,
Some few there are to whom thy radiant smile
  Is better than a thousand victories,
Though all the nobly slain of Waterloo
Rise up in wrath against them! tarry still, there are a
    few

Who for thy sake would give their manlihood
  And consecrate their being, I at least
Have done so, made thy lips my daily food,
  And in thy temples found a goodlier feast
Than this starved age can give me, spite of all
Its new-found creeds so sceptical and so dogmatical.

Here not Cephissos, not Ilissos flows,
  The woods of white Colonos are not here,
On our bleak hills the olive never blows,
  No simple priest conducts his lowing steer
Up the steep marble way, nor through the town
Do laughing maidens bear to thee the crocus-flowered
    gown.

Yet tarry! for the boy who loved thee best,
  Whose very name should be a memory
To make thee linger, sleeps in silent rest
  Beneath the Roman walls, and melody
Still mourns her sweetest lyre, none can play
The lute of Adonais, with his lips Song passed away.

Nay, when Keats died the Muses still had left
  One silver voice to sing his threnody,
But ah! too soon of it we were bereft

When on that riven night and stormy sea
Panthea claimed her singer as her own,
And slew the mouth that praised her; since which time
    we walk alone,

Save for that fiery heart, that morning star
    Of re-arisen England, whose clear eye
Saw from our tottering throne and waste of war
    The grand Greek limbs of young Democracy
Rise mightily like Hesperus and bring
The great Republic! him at least thy love hath taught to
    sing,

And he hath been with thee at Thessaly,
    And seen white Atalanta fleet of foot
In passionless and fierce virginity
    Hunting the tuskéd boar, his honied lute
Hath pierced the cavern of the hollow hill,
And Venus laughs to know one knee will bow before
    her still.

And he hath kissed the lips of Proserpine,
    And sung the Galilæan's requiem,
That wounded forehead dashed with blood and wine
    He hath discrowned, the Ancient Gods in him
Have found their last, most ardent worshipper,
And the new Sign grows grey and dim before its
    conqueror.

Spirit of Beauty! tarry with us still,
    It is not quenched the torch of poesy,
The star that shook above the Eastern hill
    Holds unassailed its argent armoury

From all the gathering gloom and fretful fight—
O tarry with us still! for through the long and
   common night,

Morris, our sweet and simple Chaucer's child,
  Dear heritor of Spenser's tuneful reed,
With soft and sylvan pipe has oft beguiled
  The weary soul of man in troublous need,
And from the far and flowerless fields of ice
Has brought fair flowers meet to make an earthly
   paradise.

We know them all, Gudrun the strong men's bride,
  Aslaug and Olafson we know them all,
How giant Grettir fought and Sigurd died,
  And what enchantment held the king in thrall
When lonely Brynhild wrestled with the powers
That war against all passion, ah! how oft through
   summer hours,

Long listless summer hours when the noon
  Being enamoured of a damask rose
Forgets to journey westward, till the moon
  The pale usurper of its tribute grows
From a thin sickle to a silver shield
And chides its loitering car – how oft, in some cool
   grassy field

Far from the cricket-ground and noisy eight,
  At Bagley, where the rustling bluebells come
Almost before the blackbird finds a mate
  And overstay the swallow, and the hum
Of many murmuring bees flits through the leaves,
Have I lain poring on the dreamy tales his fancy
   weaves,

And through their unreal woes and mimic pain
  Wept for myself, and so was purified,
And in their simple mirth grew glad again;
  For as I sailed upon that pictured tide
The strength and splendour of the storm was mine
Without the storm's red ruin, for the singer is divine,

The little laugh of water falling down
  Is not so musical, the clammy gold
Close hoarded in the tiny waxen town
  Has less of sweetness in it, and the old
Half-withered reeds that waved in Arcady
Touched by his lips break forth again to fresher
    harmony.

Spirit of Beauty tarry yet a-while!
  Although the cheating merchants of the mart
With iron roads profane our lovely isle,
  And break on whirling wheels the limbs of Art,
Ay! though the crowded factories beget
The blind-worm Ignorance that slays the soul, O tarry
    yet!

For One at least there is, – He bears his name
  From Dante and the seraph Gabriel,—
Whose double laurels burn with deathless flame
  To light thine altar; He too loves thee well,
Who saw old Merlin lured in Vivien's snare,
And the white feet of angels coming down the golden
    stair,

Loves thee so well, that all the World for him
  A gorgeous-coloured vestiture must wear,
And Sorrow take a purple diadem,

Or else be no more Sorrow, and Despair
Gild its own thorns, and Pain, like Adon, be
Even in anguish beautiful; – such is the empery

Which Painters hold, and such the heritage
  This gentle solemn Spirit doth possess,
Being a better mirror of his age
  In all his pity, love, and weariness,
Than those who can but copy common things,
And leave the Soul unpainted with its mighty
    questionings.

But they are few, and all romance has flown,
  And men can prophesy about the sun,
And lecture on his arrows – how, alone,
  Through a waste void the soulless atoms run,
How from each tree its weeping nymph has fled,
And that no more 'mid English reeds a Naïad shows
    her head.

Methinks these new Actæons boast too soon
  That they have spied on beauty; what if we
Have analyzed the rainbow, robbed the moon
  Of her most ancient, chastest mystery,
Shall I, the last Endymion, lose all hope
Because rude eyes peer at my mistress through a
    telescope!

What profit if this scientific age
  Burst through our gates with all its retinue
Of modern miracles! Can it assuage
  One lover's breaking heart? what can it do
To make one life more beautiful, one day
More god-like in its period? but now the Age of Clay

Returns in horrid cycle, and the earth
  Hath borne again a noisy progeny
Of ignorant Titans, whose ungodly birth
  Hurls them against the august hierarchy
Which sat upon Olympus, to the Dust
They have appealed, and to that barren arbiter they
    must

Repair for judgment, let them, if they can,
  From Natural Warfare and insensate Chance,
Create the new Ideal rule for man!
  Methinks that was not my inheritance;
For I was nurtured otherwise, my soul
Passes from higher heights of life to a more supreme
    goal.

Lo! while we spake the earth did turn away
  Her visage from the God, and Hecate's boat
Rose silver-laden, till the jealous day
  Blew all its torches out: I did not note
The waning hours, to young Endymions
Time's palsied fingers count in vain his rosary of suns!

Mark how the yellow iris wearily
  Leans back its throat, as though it would be kissed
By its false chamberer, the dragon-fly,
  Who, like a blue vein on a girl's white wrist,
Sleeps on that snowy primrose of the night,
Which 'gins to flush with crimson shame, and die
    beneath the light.

Come let us go, against the pallid shield
  Of the wan sky the almond blossoms gleam,
The corn-crake nested in the unmown field
  Answers its mate, across the misty stream
On fitful wing the startled curlews fly,
And in his sedgy bed the lark, for joy that Day is nigh,

Scatters the pearléd dew from off the grass,
  In tremulous ecstasy to greet the sun,
Who soon in gilded panoply will pass
  Forth from yon orange-curtained pavilion
Hung in the burning east, see, the red rim
O'ertops the expectant hills! it is the God! for love of
    him

Already the shrill lark is out of sight,
  Flooding with waves of song this silent dell,—
Ah! there is something more in that bird's flight
  Than could be tested in a crucible!—
But the air freshens, let us go, why soon
The woodmen will be here; how we have lived this
    night of June!

La Bella Donna Della Mia Mente

My limbs are wasted with a flame,
  My feet are sore with travelling,
For calling on my Lady's name
  My lips have now forgot to sing.

O Linnet in the wild-rose brake
  Strain for my Love thy melody,
O Lark sing louder for love's sake,
  My gentle Lady passeth by.

She is too fair for any man
  To see or hold his heart's delight,
Fairer than Queen or courtezan
  Or moon-lit water in the night.

Her hair is bound with myrtle leaves,
  (Green leaves upon her golden hair!)
Green grasses through the yellow sheaves
  Of autumn corn are not more fair.

Her little lips, more made to kiss
  Than to cry bitterly for pain,
Are tremulous as brook-water is,
  Or roses after evening rain.

Her neck is like white melilote
  Flushing for pleasure of the sun,
The throbbing of the linnet's throat
  Is not so sweet to look upon.

As a pomegranate, cut in twain,
  White-seeded, is her crimson mouth,
Her cheeks are as the fading stain
  Where the peach reddens to the south.

O twining hands! O delicate
  White body made for love and pain!
O House of love! O desolate
  Pale flower beaten by the rain!

By The Arno

The oleander on the wall
Grows crimson in the dawning light,
Though the grey shadows of the night
Lie yet on Florence like a pall.

The dew is bright upon the hill,
And bright the blossoms overhead,
But ah! the grasshoppers have fled,
The little Attic song is still.

Only the leaves are gently stirred
By the soft breathing of the gale,
And in the almond-scented vale
The lonely nightingale is heard.

The day will make thee silent soon,
O nightingale sing on for love!
While yet upon the shadowy grove
Splinter the arrows of the moon.

Before across the silent lawn
In sea-green vest the morning steals,
And to love's frightened eyes reveals
The long white fingers of the dawn

Fast climbing up the eastern sky
To grasp and slay the shuddering night,
All careless of my heart's delight,
Or if the nightingale should die.

Charmides

I

He was a Grecian lad, who coming home
  With pulpy figs and wine from Sicily
Stood at his galley's prow, and let the foam
  Blow through his crisp brown curls unconsciously,
And holding wave and wind in boy's despite
Peered from his dripping seat across the wet and
    stormy night

Till with the dawn he saw a burnished spear
  Like a thin thread of gold against the sky,
And hoisted sail, and strained the creaking gear,
  And bade the pilot head her lustily
Against the nor'west gale, and all day long
Held on his way, and marked the rowers' time with
    measured song,

And when the faint Corinthian hills were red
  Dropped anchor in a little sandy bay,
And with fresh boughs of olive crowned his head,
  And brushed from cheek and throat the hoary spray,
And washed his limbs with oil, and from the hold
Brought out his linen tunic and his sandals brazen-
    soled,

And a rich robe stained with the fishes' juice
  Which of some swarthy trader he had bought
Upon the sunny quay at Syracuse,
  And was with Tyrian broideries inwrought,
And by the questioning merchants made his way
Up through the soft and silver woods, and when the
    labouring day

Had spun its tangled web of crimson cloud,
  Clomb the high hill, and with swift silent feet
Crept to the fane unnoticed by the crowd
  Of busy priests, and from some dark retreat
Watched the young swains his frolic playmates bring
The firstling of their little flock, and the shy shepherd
    fling

The crackling salt upon the flame, or hang
  His studded crook against the temple wall
To Her who keeps away the ravenous fang
  Of the base wolf from homestead and from stall;
And then the clear-voiced maidens 'gan to sing,
And to the altar each man brought some goodly
    offering,

A beechen cup brimming with milky foam,
  A fair cloth wrought with cunning imagery
Of hounds in chase, a waxen honey-comb
  Dripping with oozy gold which scarce the bee
Had ceased from building, a black skin of oil
Meet for the wrestlers, a great boar the fierce and
    white-tusked spoil

Stolen from Artemis that jealous maid
  To please Athena, and the dappled hide
Of a tall stag who in some mountain glade
  Had met the shaft; and then the herald cried,
And from the pillared precinct one by one
Went the glad Greeks well pleased that they their
    simple vows had done.

And the old priest put out the waning fires
  Save that one lamp whose restless ruby glowed
For ever in the cell, and the shrill lyres

Came fainter on the wind, as down the road
In joyous dance these country folk did pass,
And with stout hands the warder closed the gates of
　　polished brass.

Long time he lay and hardly dared to breathe,
　And heard the cadenced drip of spilt-out wine,
And the rose-petals falling from the wreath
　As the night breezes wandered through the shrine,
And seemed to be in some entrancèd swoon
Till through the open roof above the full and
　　brimming moon

Flooded with sheeny waves the marble floor,
　When from his nook upleapt the venturous lad,
And flinging wide the cedar-carven door
　Beheld an awful image saffron-clad
And armed for battle! the gaunt Griffin glared
From the huge helm, and the long lance of wreck and
　　ruin flared

Like a red rod of flame, stony and steeled
　The Gorgon's head its leaden eyeballs rolled,
And writhed its snaky horrors through the shield,
　And gaped aghast with bloodless lips and cold
In passion impotent, while with blind gaze
The blinking owl between the feet hooted in shrill
　　amaze.

The lonely fisher as he trimmed his lamp
　Far out at sea off Sunium, or cast
The net for tunnies, heard a brazen tramp
　Of horses smite the waves, and a wild blast

Divide the folded curtains of the night,
And knelt upon the little poop, and prayed in holy
    fright.

And guilty lovers in their venery
  Forgat a little while their stolen sweets,
Deeming they heard dread Dian's bitter cry;
  And the grim watchmen on their lofty seats
Ran to their shields in haste precipitate,
Or strained black-bearded throats across the dusky
    parapet.

For round the temple rolled the clang of arms,
  And the twelve Gods leapt up in marble fear,
And the air quaked with dissonant alarums
  Till huge Poseidon shook his mighty spear,
And on the frieze the prancing horses neighed,
And the low tread of hurrying feet rang from the
    cavalcade.

Ready for death with parted lips he stood,
  And well content at such a price to see
That calm wide brow, that terrible maidenhood,
  The marvel of that pitiless chastity,
Ah! well content indeed, for never wight
Since Troy's young shepherd prince had seen so
    wonderful a sight.

Ready for death he stood, but lo! the air
  Grew silent, and the horses ceased to neigh,
And off his brow he tossed the clustering hair,
  And from his limbs he threw the cloak away,
For whom would not such love make desperate,
And nigher came, and touched her throat, and with
    hands violate

Undid the cuirass, and the crocus gown,
  And bared the breasts of polished ivory,
Till from the waist the peplos falling down
  Left visible the secret mystery
Which to no lover will Athena show,
The grand cool flanks, the crescent thighs, the bossy
    hills of snow.

A little space he let his greedy eyes
  Rest on the burnished image, till mere sight
Half swooned for surfeit of such luxuries,
  And then his lips in hungering delight
Fed on her lips, and round the towered neck
He flung his arms, nor cared at all his passion's will to
    check.

Never I ween did lover hold such tryst,
  For all night long he murmured honeyed word,
And saw her sweet unravished limbs, and kissed
  Her pale and argent body undisturbed,
And paddled with the polished throat, and pressed
His hot and beating heart upon her chill and icy breast.

It was as if Numidian javelins
  Pierced through and through his wild and whirling
    brain,
And his nerves thrilled like throbbing violins
  In exquisite pulsation, and the pain
Was such sweet anguish that he never drew
His lips from hers till overhead the lark of warning
    flew.

The moon was girdled with a crystal rim,
  The sign which shipmen say is ominous
Of wrath in heaven, the wan stars were dim,
  And the low lightening east was tremulous
With the faint fluttering wings of flying dawn,
Ere from the silent sombre shrine this lover had
    withdrawn.

Down the steep rock with hurried feet and fast
  Clomb the brave lad, and reached the cave of Pan,
And heard the goat-foot snoring as he passed,
  And leapt upon a grassy knoll and ran
Like a young fawn unto an olive wood
Which in a shady valley by the well-built city stood.

And sought a little stream, which well he knew,
  For oftentimes with boyish careless shout
The green and crested grebe he would pursue,
  Or snare in woven net the silver trout,
And down amid the startled reeds he lay
Panting in breathless sweet affright, and waited for the
    day.

On the green bank he lay, and let one hand
  Dip in the cool dark eddies listlessly,
And soon the breath of morning came and fanned
  His hot flushed cheeks, or lifted wantonly
The tangled curls from off his forehead, while
He on the running water gazed with strange and secret
    smile.

And soon the shepherd in rough woollen cloak
  With his long crook undid the wattled cotes,
And from the stack a thin blue wreath of smoke

Curled through the air across the ripening oats,
And on the hill the yellow house-dog bayed
As through the crisp and rustling fern the heavy cattle
    strayed.

And when the light-foot mower went afield
    Across the meadows laced with threaded dew,
And the sheep bleated on the misty weald,
    And from its nest the waking corn-crake flew,
Some woodmen saw him lying by the stream
And marvelled much that any lad so beautiful could
    seem,

Nor deemed him born of mortals, and one said,
    'It is young Hylas, that false runaway
Who with a Naïad now would make his bed
    Forgetting Herakles,' but others, 'Nay,
It is Narcissus, his own paramour,
Those are the fond and crimson lips no woman can
    allure.'

And when they nearer came a third one cried,
    'It is young Dionysos who has hid
His spear and fawnskin by the river side
    Weary of hunting with the Bassarid,
And wise indeed were we away to fly
They live not long who on the gods immortal come to
    spy.'

So turned they back, and feared to look behind,
    And told the timid swain how they had seen
Amid the reeds some woodland God reclined,

And no man dared to cross the open green,
And on that day no olive-tree was slain,
Nor rushes cut, but all deserted was the fair domain.

Save when the neat-herd's lad, his empty pail
  Well slung upon his back, with leap and bound
Raced on the other side, and stopped to hail
  Hoping that he some comrade new had found,
And gat no answer, and then half afraid
Passed on his simple way, or down the still and silent
    glade

A little girl ran laughing from the farm
  Not thinking of love's secret mysteries,
And when she saw the white and gleaming arm
  And all his manlihood, with longing eyes
Whose passion mocked her sweet virginity
Watched him a-while, and then stole back sadly and
    wearily.

Far off he heard the city's hum and noise,
  And now and then the shriller laughter where
The passionate purity of brown-limbed boys
  Wrestled or raced in the clear healthful air,
And now and then a little tinkling bell
As the shorn wether led the sheep down to the mossy
    well.

Through the grey willows danced the fretful gnat,
  The grasshopper chirped idly from the tree,
In sleek and oily coat the water-rat
  Breasting the little ripples manfully

Made for the wild-duck's nest, from bough to bough
Hopped the shy finch, and the huge tortoise crept
   across the slough.

On the faint wind floated the silky seeds
  As the bright scythe swept through the waving grass,
The ousel-cock splashed circles in the reeds
  And flecked with silver whorls the forest's glass,
Which scare had caught again its imagery
Ere from its bed the dusky tench leapt at the dragon-
   fly.

But little care had he for any thing
  Though up and down the beech the squirrel played,
And from the copse the linnet 'gan to sing
  To her brown mate her sweetest serenade,
Ah! little care indeed, for he had seen
The breasts of Pallas and the naked wonder of the
   Queen.

But when the herdsman called his straggling goats
  With whistling pipe across the rocky road,
And the shard-beetle with its trumpet-notes
  Boomed through the darkening woods, and seemed to
   bode
Of coming storm, and the belated crane
Passed homeward like a shadow, and the dull big
   drops of rain

Fell on the pattering fig-leaves, up he rose,
  And from the gloomy forest went his way
Past sombre homestead and wet orchard-close,
  And came at last unto a little quay,

And called his mates a-board, and took his seat
On the high poop, and pushed from land, and loosed
   the dripping sheet,

And steered across the bay, and when nine suns
  Passed down the long and laddered way of gold,
And nine pale moons had breathed their orisons
  To the chaste stars their confessors, or told
Their dearest secret to the downy moth
That will not fly at noonday, through the foam and
   surging froth

Came a great owl with yellow sulphurous eyes
  And lit upon the ship, whose timbers creaked
As though the lading of three argosies
  Were in the hold, and flapped its wings, and
   shrieked,
And darkness straightway stole across the deep,
Sheathed was Orion's sword, dread Mars himself fled
   down the steep,

And the moon hid behind a tawny mask
  Of drifting cloud, and from the ocean's marge
Rose the red plume, the huge and hornèd casque,
  The seven-cubit spear, the brazen targe!
And clad in bright and burnished panoply
Athena strode across the stretch of sick and shivering
   sea!

To the dull sailors' sight her loosened locks
  Seemed like the jagged storm-rack, and her feet
Only the spume that floats on hidden rocks,
  And, marking how the rising waters beat

Against the rolling ship, the pilot cried
To the young helmsman at the stern to luff to
    windward side.

But he, the over-bold adulterer,
  A dear profaner of great mysteries,
An ardent amorous idolater,
  When he beheld those grand relentless eyes
Laughed loud for joy, and crying out 'I come'
Leapt from the lofty poop into the chill and churning
    foam.

Then fell from the high heaven one bright star,
  One dancer left the circling galaxy,
And back to Athens on her clattering car
  In all the pride of venged divinity
Pale Pallas swept with shrill and steely clank,
And a few gurgling bubbles rose where her boy lover
    sank.

And the mast shuddered as the gaunt owl flew
  With mocking hoots after the wrathful Queen,
And the old pilot bade the trembling crew
  Hoist the big sail, and told how he had seen
Close to the stern a dim and giant form,
And like a dipping swallow the stout ship dashed
    through the storm.

And no man dared to speak of Charmides
  Deeming that he some evil thing had wrought,
And when they reached the strait Symplegades
  They beached their galley on the shore, and sought
The toll-gate of the city hastily,
And in the market showed their brown and pictured
    pottery.

II

But some good Triton-god had ruth, and bare
  The boy's drowned body back to Grecian land,
And mermaids combed his dank and dripping hair
  And smoothed his brow, and loosed his clenching
    hand,
Some brought sweet spices from far Araby,
And others bade the halcyon sing her softest lullaby.

And when he neared his old Athenian home,
  A mighty billow rose up suddenly
Upon whose oily back the clotted foam
  Lay diapered in some strange fantasy,
And clasping him unto its glassy breast,
Swept landward, like a white-maned steed upon a
    venturous quest!

Now where Colonos leans unto the sea
  There lies a long and level stretch of lawn,
The rabbit knows it, and the mountain bee
  For it deserts Hymettus, and the Faun
Is not afraid, for never through the day
Comes a cry ruder than the shout of shepherd lads at
    play.

But often from the thorny labyrinth
  And tangled branches of the circling wood
The stealthy hunter sees young Hyacinth
  Hurling the polished disk, and draws his hood
Over his guilty gaze, and creeps away,
Nor dares to wind his horn, or – else at the first break
    of day

The Dryads come and throw the leathern ball
  Along the reedy shore, and circumvent
Some goat-eared Pan to be their seneschal
  For fear of bold Poseidon's ravishment,
And loose their girdles, with shy timorous eyes,
Lest from the surf his azure arms and purple beard
    should rise.

On this side and on that a rocky cave,
  Hung with the yellow-bell'd laburnum, stands,
Smooth is the beach, save where some ebbing wave
  Leaves its faint outline etched upon the sands,
As though it feared to be too soon forgot
By the green rush, its playfellow, – and yet, it is a spot

So small, that the inconstant butterfly
  Could steal the hoarded honey from each flower
Ere it was noon, and still not satisfy
  Its over-greedy love, – within an hour
A sailor boy, were he but rude enow
To land and pluck a garland for his galley's painted
    prow,

Would almost leave the little meadow bare,
  For it knows nothing of great pageantry,
Only a few narcissi here and there
  Stand separate in sweet austerity,
Dotting the unmown grass with silver stars,
And here and there a daffodil waves tiny scimetars.

Hither the billow brought him, and was glad
  Of such dear servitude, and where the land
Was virgin of all waters laid the lad
  Upon the golden margent of the strand,

And like a lingering lover oft returned
To kiss those pallid limbs which once with intense fire
   burned,

Ere the wet seas had quenched that holocaust,
   That self-fed flame, that passionate lustihead,
Ere grisly death with chill and nipping frost
   Had withered up those lilies white and red
Which, while the boy would through the forest range,
Answered each other in a sweet antiphonal counter-
   change.

And when at dawn the woodnymphs, hand-in-hand,
   Threaded the bosky dell, their satyr spied
The boy's pale body stretched upon the sand,
   And feared Poseidon's treachery, and cried,
And like bright sunbeams flitting through a glade,
Each startled Dryad sought some safe and leafy
   ambuscade.

Save one white girl, who deemed it would not be
   So dread a thing to feel a sea-god's arms
Crushing her breasts in amorous tyranny,
   And longed to listen to those subtle charms
Insidious lovers weave when they would win
Some fencèd fortress, and stole back again, nor thought
   it sin

To yield her treasure unto one so fair,
   And lay beside him, thirsty with love's drouth,
Called him soft names, played with his tangled hair,
   And with hot lips made havoc of his mouth

Afraid he might not wake, and then afraid
Lest he might wake too soon, fled back, and then, fond
   renegade,

Returned to fresh assault, and all day long
  Sat at his side, and laughed at her new toy,
And held his hand, and sang her sweetest song,
  Then frowned to see how froward was the boy
Who would not with her maidenhood entwine,
Nor knew that three days since his eyes had looked on
   Proserpine,

Nor knew what sacrilege his lips had done,
  But said, 'He will awake, I know him well,
He will awake at evening when the sun
  Hangs his red shield on Corinth's citadel,
This sleep is but a cruel treachery
To make me love him more, and in some cavern of
   the sea

Deeper than ever falls the fisher's line
  Already a huge Triton blows his horn,
And weaves a garland from the crystalline
  And drifting ocean-tendrils to adorn
The emerald pillars of our bridal bed,
For sphered in foaming silver, and with coral-crownèd
   head,

We two will sit upon a throne of pearl,
  And a blue wave will be our canopy,
And at our feet the water-snakes will curl
  In all their amethystine panoply
Of diamonded mail, and we will mark
The mullets swimming by the mast of some storm-
   foundered bark,

Vermilion-finned with eyes of bossy gold
  Like flakes of crimson light, and the great deep
His glassy-portaled chamber will unfold,
  And we will see the painted dolphins sleep
Cradled by murmuring halcyons on the rocks
Where Proteus in quaint suit of green pastures his
    monstrous flocks.

And tremulous opal-hued anemones
  Will wave their purple fringes where we tread
Upon the mirrored floor, and argosies
  Of fishes flecked with tawny scales will thread
The drifting cordage of the shattered wreck,
And honey-coloured amber beads our twining limbs
    will deck.'

But when that baffled Lord of War the Sun
  With gaudy pennon flying passed away
Into his brazen House, and one by one
  The little yellow stars began to stray
Across the field of heaven, ah! then indeed
She feared his lips upon her lips would never care to
    feed,

And cried, 'Awake, already the pale moon
  Washes the trees with silver, and the wave
Creeps grey and chilly up this sandy dune,
  The croaking frogs are out, and from the cave
The night-jar shrieks, the fluttering bats repass,
And the brown stoat with hollow flanks creeps through
    the dusky grass.

Nay, though thou art a God, be not so coy,
　For in yon stream there is a little reed
That often whispers how a lovely boy
　Lay with her once upon a grassy mead,
Who when his cruel pleasure he had done
Spread wings of rustling gold and soared aloft into the
　　sun.

Be not so coy, the laurel trembles still
　With great Apollo's kisses, and the fir
Whose clustering sisters fringe the sea-ward hill
　Hath many a tale of that bold ravisher
Whom men call Boreas, and I have seen
The mocking eyes of Hermes through the poplar's
　　silvery sheen.

Even the jealous Naiads call me fair,
　And every morn a young and ruddy swain
Woos me with apples and with locks of hair,
　And seeks to soothe my virginal disdain
By all the gifts the gentle wood-nymphs love;
But yesterday he brought to me an iris-plumaged dove

With little crimson feet, which with its store
　Of seven spotted eggs the cruel lad
Had stolen from the lofty sycamore
　At day-break, when her amorous comrade had
Flown off in search of berried juniper
Which most they love; the fretful wasp, that earliest
　　vintager

Of the blue grapes, hath not persistency
　So constant as this simple shepherd-boy
For my poor lips, his joyous purity

And laughing sunny eyes might well decoy
A Dryad from her oath to Artemis;
For very beautiful is he, his mouth was made to kiss,

His argent forehead, like a rising moon
  Over the dusky hills of meeting brows,
Is crescent shaped, the hot and Tyrian noon
  Leads from the myrtle-grove no goodlier spouse
For Cytheræa, the first silky down
Fringes his blushing cheeks, and his young limbs are
    strong and brown:

And he is rich, and fat and fleecy herds
  Of bleating sheep upon his meadows lie,
And many an earthern bowl of yellow curds
  Is in his homestead for the thievish fly
To swim and drown in, the pink clover mead
Keeps its sweet store for him, and he can pipe on
    oaten reed.

And yet I love him not, it was for thee
  I kept my love, I knew that thou would'st come
To rid me of this pallid chastity;
  Thou fairest flower of the flowerless foam
Of all the wide Ægean, brightest star
Of ocean's azure heavens where the mirrored planets
    are!

I knew that thou would'st come, for when at first
  The dry wood burgeoned, and the sap of Spring
Swelled in my green and tender bark or burst
  To myriad multitudinous blossoming
Which mocked the midnight with its mimic moons
That did not dread the dawn, and first the thrushes'
    rapturous tunes

Startled the squirrel from its granary,
  And cuckoo flowers fringed the narrow lane,
Through my young leaves a sensuous ecstasy
  Crept like new wine, and every mossy vein
Throbbed with the fitful pulse of amorous blood,
And the wild winds of passion shook my slim stem's
    maidenhood.

The trooping fawns at evening came and laid
  Their cool black noses on my lowest boughs,
And on my topmost branch the blackbird made
  A little nest of grasses for his spouse,
And now and then a twittering wren would light
On a thin twig which hardly bare the weight of such
    delight.

I was the Attic shepherd's trysting place,
  Beneath my shadow Amaryllis lay,
And round my trunk would laughing Daphnis chase
  The timorous girl, till tired out with play
She felt his hot breath stir her tangled hair,
And turned, and looked, and fled no more from such
    delightful snare.

Then come away unto my ambuscade
  Where clustering woodbine weaves a canopy
For amorous pleasaunce, and the rustling shade
  Of Paphian myrtles seems to sanctify
The dearest rites of love, there in the cool
And green recesses of its farthest depth there is a pool,

The ouzel's haunt, the wild bee's pasturage,
  For round its rim great creamy lilies float
Through their flat leaves in verdant anchorage,

Each cup a white-sailed golden-laden boat
Steered by a dragon-fly, — be not afraid
To leave this wan and wave-kissed shore, surely the
    place was made

For lovers such as we, the Cyprian Queen,
  One arm around her boyish paramour,
Strays often there at eve, and I have seen
  The moon strip off her misty vestiture
For young Endymion's eyes, be not afraid,
The panther feet of Dian never tread that secret glade.

Nay if thou wil'st, back to the beating brine,
  Back to the boisterous billow let us go,
And walk all day beneath the hyaline
  Huge vault of Neptune's watery portico,
And watch the purple monsters of the deep
Sport in ungainly play, and from his lair keen Xiphias
    leap.

For if my mistress find me lying here
  She will not ruth or gentle pity show,
But lay her boar-spear down, and with austere
  Relentless fingers string the cornel bow,
And draw the feathered notch against her breast,
And loose the archèd cord, ay, even now upon the
    quest

I hear her hurrying feet, — awake, awake,
  Thou laggard in love's battle! once at least
Let me drink deep of passion's wine, and slake
  My parchèd being with the nectarous feast

Which even Gods affect! O come Love come,
Still we have time to reach the cavern of thine azure
   home.'

Scarce had she spoken when the shuddering trees
   Shook, and the leaves divided, and the air
Grew conscious of a God, and the grey seas
   Crawled backward, and a long and dismal blare
Blew from some tasselled horn, a sleuth-hound bayed,
And like a flame a barbèd reed flew whizzing down
   the glade.

And where the little flowers of her breast
   Just brake into their milky blossoming,
This murderous paramour, this unbidden guest,
   Pierced and struck deep in horrid chambering,
And ploughed a bloody furrow with its dart,
And dug a long red road, and cleft with wingèd death
   her heart.

Sobbing her life out with a bitter cry
   On the boy's body fell the Dryad maid,
Sobbing for incomplete virginity,
   And raptures unenjoyed, and pleasures dead,
And all the pain of things unsatisfied,
And the bright drops of crimson youth crept down her
   throbbing side.

Ah! pitiful it was to hear her moan,
   And very pitiful to see her die
Ere she had yielded up her sweets, or known
   The joy of passion, that dread mystery
Which not to know is not to live at all,
And yet to know is to be held in death's most deadly
   thrall.

But as it hapt the Queen of Cythere,
  Who with Adonis all night long had lain
Within some shepherd's hut in Arcady,
On team of silver doves and gilded wane
  Was journeying Paphos-ward, high up afar
From mortal ken between the mountains and the
    morning star,

And when low down she spied the hapless pair,
  And heard the Oread's faint despairing cry,
Whose cadence seemed to play upon the air
  As though it were a viol, hastily
She bade her pigeons fold each straining plume,
And dropt to earth and reached the strand, and saw
    their dolorous doom.

For as a gardener turning back his head
  To catch the last notes of the linnet, mows
With careless scythe too near some flower bed,
  And cuts the thorny pillar of the rose,
And with the flower's loosened loveliness
Strews the brown mould, or as some shepherd lad in
    wantonness

Driving his little flock along the mead
  Treads down two daffodils which side by side
Have lured the lady-bird with yellow brede
  And made the gaudy moth forget its pride,
Treads down their brimming golden chalices
Under light feet which were not made for such rude
    ravages,

Or as a schoolboy tired of his book
  Flings himself down upon the reedy grass
And plucks two water-lilies from the brook,
  And for a time forgets the hour glass,
Then wearies of their sweets, and goes his way,
And lets the hot sun kill them, even so these lovers lay.

And Venus cried, 'It is dread Artemis
  Whose bitter hand hath wrought this cruelty,
Or else that mightier maid whose care it is
  To guard her strong and stainless majesty
Upon the hill Athenian, – alas!
That they who loved so well unloved into Death's
    house should pass.

So with soft hands she laid the boy and girl
  In the great golden waggon tenderly,
Her white throat whiter than a moony pearl
  Just threaded with a blue vein's tapestry
Had not yet ceased to throb, and still her breast
Swayed like a wind-stirred lily in ambiguous unrest.

And then each pigeon spread its milky van,
  The bright car soared into the dawning sky,
And like a cloud the aerial caravan
  Passed over the Ægean silently,
Till the faint air was troubled with the song
From the wan mouths that call on bleeding Thammuz
    all night long.

But when the doves had reached their wonted goal
  Where the wide stair of orbèd marble dips
Its snows into the sea, her fluttering soul
  Just shook the trembling petals of her lips

And passed into the void, and Venus knew
That one fair maid the less would walk amid her
    retinue,

And bade her servants carve a cedar chest
  With all the wonder of this history,
Within whose scented womb their limbs should rest
  Where olive-trees make tender the blue sky
On the low hills of Paphos, and the faun
Pipes in the noonday, and the nightingale sings on till
    dawn.

Nor failed they to obey her hest, and ere
  The morning bee had stung the daffodil
With tiny fretful spear, or from its lair
  The waking stag had leapt across the rill
And roused the ouzel, or the lizard crept
Athwart the sunny rock, beneath the grass their bodies
    slept.

And when day brake, within that silver shrine
  Fed by the flames of cressets tremulous,
Queen Venus knelt and prayed to Proserpine
  That she whose beauty made Death amorous
Should beg a guerdon from her pallid Lord,
And let Desire pass across dread Charon's icy ford.

III

In melancholy moonless Acheron,
  Far from the goodly earth and joyous day,
Where no spring ever buds, nor ripening sun
  Weighs down the apple trees, nor flowery May

Chequers with chestnut blooms the grassy floor,
Where thrushes never sing, and piping linnets mate no
  more,

There by a dim and dark Lethæan well
  Young Charmides was lying, wearily
He plucked the blossoms from the asphodel,
  And with its little rifled treasury
Strewed the dull waters of the dusky stream,
And watched the white stars founder, and the land was
    like a dream,

When as he gazed into the watery glass
  And through his brown hair's curly tangles scanned
His own wan face, a shadow seemed to pass
  Across the mirror, and a little hand
Stole into his, and warm lips timidly
Brushed his pale cheeks, and breathed their secret forth
    into a sigh.

Then turned he round his weary eyes and saw,
  And ever nigher still their faces came,
And nigher ever did their young mouths draw
  Until they seemed one perefect rose of flame,
And longing arms around her neck he cast,
And felt her throbbing bosom, and his breath came hot
    and fast,

And all his hoarded sweets were hers to kiss,
  And all her maidenhood was his to slay,
And limb to limb in long and rapturous bliss
  Their passion waxed and waned, − O why essay
To pipe again of love too venturous reed!
Enough, enough that Erôs laughed upon that flowerless
    mead.

Too venturous poesy O why essay
  To pipe again of passion! fold thy wings
O'er daring Icarus and bid thy lay
  Sleep hidden in the lyre's silent strings,
  Till thou hast found the old Castalian rill,
Or from the Lesbian waters plucked drowned Sappho's
    golden quill!

Enough, enough that he whose life had been
  A fiery pulse of sin, a splendid shame,
Could in the loveless land of Hades glean
  One scorching harvest from those fields of flame
Where passion walks with naked unshod feet
And is not wounded, – ah! enough that once their lips
    could meet

In that wild throb when all existences
  Seem narrowed to one single ecstasy
Which dies through its own sweetness and the stress
  Of too much pleasure, ere Persephone
Had bade them serve her by the ebon throne
Of the pale God who in the fields of Enna loosed her
    zone.

Athanasia

To that gaunt House of Art which lacks for naught
  Of all the great things men have saved from Time,
The withered body of a girl was brought
  Dead ere the world's glad youth had touched its
prime,
And seen by lonely Arabs lying hid
In the dim womb of some black pyramid.

But when they had unloosed the linen band
  Which swathed the Egyptian's body, – lo! was found
Closed in the wasted hollow of her hand
  A little seed, which sown in English ground
Did wondrous snow of starry blossoms bear,
And spread rich odours through our springtide air.

With such strange arts this flower did allure
  That all forgotten was the asphodel,
And the brown bee, the lily's paramour,
  Forsook the cup where he was wont to dwell,
For not a thing of earth it seemed to be,
But stolen from some heavenly Arcady.

In vain the sad narcissus, wan and white
  At its own beauty, hung across the stream,
The purple dragon-fly had no delight
  With its gold dust to make his wings a-gleam,
Ah! no delight the jasmine-bloom to kiss,
Or brush the rain-pearls from the eucharis.

For love of it the passionate nightingale
  Forgot the hills of Thrace, the cruel king,
And the pale dove no longer cared to sail

Through the wet woods at time of blossoming,
But round this flower of Egypt sought to float,
With silvered wing and amethystine throat.

While the hot sun blazed in his tower of blue
  A cooling wind crept from the land of snows,
And the warm south with tender tears of dew
  Drenched its white leaves when Hesperos uprose
Amid those sea-green meadows of the sky
On which the scarlet bars of sunset lie.

But when o'er wastes of lily-haunted field
  The tired birds had stayed their amorous tune,
And broad and glittering like an argent shield
  High in the sapphire heavens hung the moon,
Did no strange dream or evil memory make
Each tremulous petal of its blossoms shake?

Ah no! to this bright flower a thousand years
  Seemed but the lingering of a summer's day,
It never knew the tide of cankering fears
  Which turn a boy's gold hair to withered grey,
The dread desire of death it never knew,
Or how all folk that they were born must rue.

For we to death with pipe and dancing go,
  Nor would we pass the ivory gate again,
As some sad river wearied of its flow
  Through the dull plains, the haunts of common men,
Leaps lover-like into the terrible sea!
And counts it gain to die so gloriously.

We mar our lordly strength in barren strife
  With the world's legions led by clamorous care,
It never feels decay but gathers life
  From the pure sunlight and the supreme air,
We live beneath Time's wasting sovereignty,
It is the child of all eternity.

Impression du Matin

The Thames nocturne of blue and gold
  Changed to a Harmony in grey:
  A barge with ochre-coloured hay
Dropt from the wharf: and chill and cold

The yellow fog came creeping down
  The bridges, till the houses' walls
  Seemed changed to shadows, and S. Paul's
Loomed like a bubble o'er the town.

Then suddenly arose the clang
  Of waking life; the streets were stirred
  With country waggons: and a bird
Flew to the glistening roofs and sang.

But one pale woman all alone,
  The daylight kissing her wan hair,
  Loitered beneath the gas lamps' flare,
With lips of flame and heart of stone.

Impression: Le Reveillon

The sky is laced with fitful red,
The circling mists and shadows flee,
The dawn is rising from the sea,
Like a white lady from her bed.

And jagged brazen arrows fall
Athwart the feathers of the night,
And a long wave of yellow light
Breaks silently on tower and hall,

And spreading wide across the wold
Wakes into flight some fluttering bird,
And all the chestnut tops are stirred,
And all the branches streaked with gold.

Impressions

I Les Silhouettes

The sea is flecked with bars of grey,
The dull dead wind is out of tune,
And like a withered leaf the moon
Is blown across the stormy bay.

Etched clear upon the pallid sand
Lies the black boat: a sailor boy
Clambers aboard in careless joy
With laughing face and gleaming hand.

And overhead the curlews cry,
Where through the dusky upland grass
The young brown-throated reapers pass,
Like silhouettes against the sky.

II La Fuite de la Lune

To outer senses there is peace,
A dreamy peace on either hand,
Deep silence in the shadowy land,
Deep silence where the shadows cease.

Save for a cry that echoes shrill
From some lone bird disconsolate;
A corn-crake calling to its mate;
The answer from the misty hill.

And suddenly the moon withdraws
Her sickle from the lightening skies,
And to her sombre cavern flies,
Wrapped in a veil of yellow gauze.

In the Gold Room *A Harmony*

Her ivory hands on the ivory keys
  Strayed in a fitful fantasy,
Like the silver gleam when the poplar trees
  Rustle their pale leaves listlessly,
  Or the drifting foam of a restless sea
When the waves show their teeth in the flying breeze.

Her gold hair fell on the wall of gold
  Like the delicate gossamer tangles spun
On the burnished disk of the marigold,
  Or the sun-flower turning to meet the sun
  When the gloom of the dark blue night is done,
And the spear of the lily is aureoled.

And her sweet red lips on these lips of mine
  Burned like the ruby fire set
In the swinging lamp of a crimson shrine,
  Or the bleeding wounds of the pomegranate,
  Or the heart of the lotus drenched and wet
With the spilt-out blood of the rose-red wine.

Impressions

I Le Jardin

The lily's withered chalice falls
  Around its rod of dusty gold,
  And from the beech trees on the wold
The last wood-pigeon coos and calls.

The gaudy leonine sunflower
  Hangs black and barren on its stalk,
  And down the wintry garden walk
The dead leaves scatter, – hour by hour.

Pale privet-petals white as milk
  Are blown into a snowy mass;
  The roses lie upon the grass,
Like little shreds of crimson silk.

II La Mer

A white mist drifts across the shrouds,
  A wild moon in this wintery sky
  Gleams like an angry lion's eye
Out of a mane of tawny clouds.

The muffled steersman at the wheel
  Is but a shadow in the gloom;—
  And in the throbbing engine room
Leap the long rods of polished steel.

The shattered storm has left its trace
  Upon this huge and heaving dome,
  For the threads of yellow foam
Float on the waves like ravelled lace.

Le Jardin des Tuileries

This winter air is keen and cold,
  And keen and cold this winter sun,
  But round my chair the children run
Like little things of dancing gold.

Sometimes about the painted kiosk
  The mimic soldiers strut and stride,
  Sometimes the blue-eyed brigands hide
In the bleak tangles of the bosk.

And sometimes, while the old nurse cons
  Her book, they steal across the square,
  And launch their paper navies where
Huge Triton writhes in greenish bronze.

And now in mimic flight they flee,
  And now they rush, a boisterous band—
  And, tiny hand on tiny hand,
Climb up the black and leafless tree.

Ah! cruel tree! if I were you,
  And children climbed me, for their sake
  Though it be winter I would break
Into Spring blossoms white and blue!

The Harlot's House

We caught the tread of dancing feet,
We loitered down the moonlit street,
And stopped beneath the Harlot's house.

Inside, above the din and fray,
We heard the loud musicians play
The 'Treues Liebes Herz', of Strauss.

Like strange mechanical grotesques,
Making fantastic arabesques,
The shadows raced across the blind.

We watched the ghostly dancers spin
To sound of horn and violin,
Like black leaves wheeling in the wind.

Like wire-pulled automatons,
Slim silhouetted skeletons
Went sidling through the slow quadrille,

Then took each other by the hand,
And danced a stately saraband;
Their laughter echoed thin and shrill.

Sometimes a clock-work puppet pressed
A phantom lover to her breast,
Sometimes they seemed to try to sing,

Sometimes a horrible Marionette
Came out, and smoked its cigarette
Upon the steps like a live thing.

Then turning to my love I said,
'The dead are dancing with the dead,
The dust is whirling with the dust.'

But she, she heard the violin,
And left my side, and entered in;
Love passed into the house of Lust.

Then suddenly the tune went false,
The dancers wearied of the waltz,
The shadows ceased to wheel and whirl,

And down the long and silent street,
The dawn with silver-sandalled feet,
Crept like a frightened girl.

On the Sale by Auction of Keats' Love Letters

These are the letters which Endymion wrote
  To one he loved in secret, and apart.
  And now the brawlers of the auction mart
Bargain and bid for each poor blotted note,
Ay! for each separate pulse of passion quote
  The merchant's price: I think they love not art,
  Who break the crystal of a poet's heart
That small and sickly eyes may glare and gloat.

Is it not said that many years ago,
  In a far Eastern town, some soldiers ran
  With torches through the midnight, and began
To wrangle for mean raiment, and to throw
  Dice for the garments of a wretched man,
Not knowing the God's wonder, or His woe!

Fantasies Décoratives

I Le Panneau

Under the rose-tree's dancing shade
  There stands a little ivory girl,
  Pulling the leaves of pink and pearl
With pale green nails of polished jade.

The red leaves fall upon the mould,
  The white leaves flutter, one by one,
  Down to a blue bowl where the sun,
Like a great dragon, writhes in gold.

The white leaves float upon the air,
  The red leaves flutter idly down,
  Some fall upon her yellow gown,
And some upon her raven hair.

She takes an amber lute and sings,
  And as she sings a silver crane
  Begins his scarlet neck to strain,
And flap his burnished metal wings.

She takes a lute of amber bright,
  And from the thicket where he lies
  Her lover, with his almond eyes,
Watches her movements in delight.

And now she gives a cry of fear,
  And tiny tears begin to start:
  A thorn has wounded with its dart
The pink-veined sea shell of her ear.

And now she laughs a merry note:
  There has fallen a petal of the rose
  Just where the yellow satin shows
The blue-veined flower of her throat.

With pale green nails of polished jade,
  Pulling the leaves of pink and pearl,
  There stands a little ivory girl
Under the rose-tree's dancing shade.

II Les Ballons

Against these turbid turquoise skies
  The light and luminous balloons
  Dip and drift like satin moons,
Drift like silken butterflies.

Reel with every windy gust,
  Rise and reel like dancing girls,
  Float like strange transparent pearls,
Fall and float like silver dust

Now to the low leaves they cling,
  Each with coy fantastic pose,
  Each a petal of a rose
Straining at a gossamer string.

Then to the tall trees they climb,
  Like thin globes of amethyst,
  Wandering opals keeping tryst
With the rubies of the lime.

Canzonet

I have no store
Of gryphon-guarded gold;
Now, as before,
Bare is the shepherd's fold.
   Rubies, nor pearls,
Have I to gem thy throat;
Yet woodland girls
Have loved the shepherd's note.

Then, pluck a reed
And bid me sing to thee,
  For I would feed
Thine ears with melody,
Who art more fair
Than fairest fleur-de-lys,
More sweet and rare
Than sweetest ambergris.

What dost thou fear?
Young Hyacinth is slain,
Pan is not here,
And will not come again.
No hornèd Faun
Treads down the yellow leas,
No God at dawn
Steals through the olive trees.

Hylas is dead,
Nor will he e'er divine
Those little red
Rose-petalled lips of thine.
On the high hill

No ivory Dryads play,
Silver and still
Sinks the sad autumn day.

Symphony in Yellow

An omnibus across the bridge
  Crawls like a yellow butterfly,
  And, here and there, a passer-by
Shows like a little restless midge.

Big barges full of yellow hay
  Are moored against the shadowy wharf,
  And, like a yellow silken scarf,
The thick fog hangs along the quay.

The yellow leaves begin to fade
  And flutter from the Temple elms,
  And at my feet the pale green Thames
Lies like a rod of rippled jade.

In the Forest

Out of the mid-woods' twilight
  Into the meadow's dawn,
Ivory-limbed and brown-eyed
  Flashes my Faun!

He skips through the copses singing,
  And his shadow dances along,
And I know not which I should follow,
  Shadow or song!

O Hunter, snare me his shadow!
  O Nightingale, catch me his strain!
Else moonstruck with music and madness
  I track him in vain.

La Circassienne

I love your tremulous topaz eyes
  That light with flame these midnight streets,
I love your body as it lies
  Like amber on the silken sheets.

I love the honey coloured hair
  That ripples to your ivory hips,
I love the tired listless air
  With which you kiss my boyish lips.

I love the wandering hyaline
  Blue vein that on your shoulder glows,
I love your pale pink nails which shine
  Like petals pilfered from the rose.

I love your mouth of vermilion,
  Your gilded breasts, your sun-scorched neck,
Which is as brown as cinnamon
  With here and there a purple fleck.

I love the bows that bend above
  Your eyelids of chalcedony,
And most of all, my love, I love,
  Your beautiful fierce chastity.

                                        Cairo.

The Sphinx

In a dim corner of my room for longer than my fancy
    thinks
A beautiful and silent Sphinx has watched me through
    the shifting gloom.

Inviolate and immobile she does not rise she does not
    stir
For silver moons are naught to her and naught to her
    the suns that reel.

Red follows grey across the air the waves of moonlight
    ebb and flow
But with the dawn she does not go and in the night-
    time she is there.

Dawn follows dawn and nights grow old and all the
    while this curious cat
Lies couching on the Chinese mat with eyes of satin
    rimmed with gold.

Upon the mat she lies and leers and on the tawny
    throat of her
Flutters the soft and silky fur or ripples to her pointed
    ears.

Come forth my lovely seneschal! so somnolent, so
    statuesque!
Come forth you exquisite grotesque! half woman and
    half animal!

Come forth my lovely languorous Sphinx! and put your
    head upon my knee!
And let me stroke your throat and seek your body
    spotted like the lynx!

And let me touch those curving claws of yellow ivory
and grasp
The tail that like a monstrous asp coils round your
heavy velvet paws!

*

A thousand weary centuries are thine while I have
hardly seen
Some twenty summers cast their green for autumn's
gaudy liveries.

But you can read the hieroglyphs on the great
sandstone obelisks,
And you have talked with Basilisks, and you have
looked on Hippogriffs.

O tell me, were you standing by when Isis to Osiris
knelt?
And did you watch the Egyptian melt her union for
Antony

And drink the jewel-drunken wine and bend her head
in mimic awe
To see the huge Proconsul draw the salted tunny from
the brine?

And did you mark the Cyprian kiss white Adon on his
catafalque?
And did you follow Amenalk, the god of Helipolis?

And did you talk with Thoth, and did you hear the
moon-horned Io weep?
And know the painted kings who sleep beneath the
wedge-shaped pyramid?

*

Lift up your large black satin eyes which are like
    cushions where one sinks!
Fawn at my feet fantastic Sphinx! and sing me all your
    memories!

Sing to me of the Jewish maid who wandered with the
    Holy Child,
And how you led them through the wild, and how
    they slept beneath your shade.

Sing to me of that odorous green eve when couching
    by the marge
You heard from Adrian's gilded barge the laughter of
    Antinous

And lapped the stream and fed your drouth and
    watched with hot and hungry stare
The ivory body of that rare young slave with his
    pomegranate mouth!

Sing to me of the labyrinth in which the twy-formed
    Bull was stalled!
Sing to me of the night you crawled across the
    temple's granite plinth

When through the purple corridors the screaming
    scarlet Ibis flew
In terror, and a horrid dew dripped from the moaning
    mandragores,

And the great torpid Crocodile within the tank shed
    slimy tears,
And tare the jewels from his ears and staggered back
    into the Nile,

And the priests cursed you with shrill psalms as in
    your claws you seized their Snake

And crept away with it to slake your passion by the
    shuddering palms!

*

Who were your lovers? who were they who wrestled
    for you in the dust?
Which was the vessel of your lust? what leman had
    you, every day?

Did giant Lizards come and crouch before you on the
    reedy banks?
Did Gryphons with great metal flanks leap on you in
    your trampled couch?

Did monstrous Hippopotami come sidling toward you
    in the mist?
Did gilt-scaled Dragons writhe and twist with passion
    as you passed them by?

And from the brick-built Lycian Tomb what horrible
    Chimaera came
With fearful heads and fearful flame to breed new
    wonders from your womb?

*

Or had you shameful secret quests and did you harry
    to your home
Some nereid coiled in amber foam with curious rock
    crystal breasts?

Or did you treading through the froth call to the
    brown Sidonian
For tidings of Leviathan, Leviathan or Behemoth?

Or did you when the sun was set climb up the cactus-
    covered slope
To meet your swarthy Ethiop whose body was of
    polished jet?

Or did you while the earthen skiffs dropped down the
    grey Nilotic flats
At twilight and the flickering bats flew round the
    Temple's triple glyphs.

Steal to the border of the bar and swim across the
    silent lake
And slink into the vault and make the pyramid your
    Lúpanar

Till from each black sarcophagus rose up the painted
    swathèd dead?
Or did you lure unto your bed the ivory-horned
    Tragelaphos?

Or did you love the God of Flies who plagued the
    Hebrews and was splashed
With wine unto the waist? Or Pasht, who had green
    beryls for her eyes?

Or that young God, the Tyrian, who was more
    amorous than the dove
Of Ashtaroth? or did you love the God of the Assyrian

Whose wings, like strange transparent talc, rose high
    above his hawk-faced head,
Painted with silver and with red and ribbed with rods
    of oreichalch?

Or did huge Apis from his car leap down and lay
    before your feet

Big blossoms of the honey-sweet and honey-coloured
   nenuphar?

*

How subtle-secret is your smile! Did you love none
then? Nay, I know
Great Ammon was your bedfellow! He lay with you
beside the Nile!

The river-horses in the slime trumpeted when they saw
him come
Odorous with Syrian galbanum and smeared with
spikenard and with thyme.

He came along the river-bank like some tall galley
argent-sailed,
He strode across the waters, mailed in beauty, and the
waters sank.

He strode across the desert sand: he reached the valley
where you lay:
He waited till the dawn of day: then touched your
black breasts with his hand.

You kissed his mouth with mouths of flame: you made
   the hornèd god your own:
You stood behind him on his throne: you called him
   by his secret name.

You whispered monstrous oracles into the caverns of
   his ears:
With blood of goats and blood of steers you taught
   him monstrous miracles.

White Ammon was your bedfellow! Your chamber was
   the steaming Nile!

And with your curved archaic smile you watched his
passion come and go.

*

With Syrian oils his brows were bright: and widespread
as a tent at noon
His marble limbs made pale the moon and lent the day
a larger light.

His long hair was nine cubits' span and coloured like
that yellow gem
Which hidden in their garment's hem the merchants
bring from Kurdistan.

His face was as the must that lies upon a vat of new-
made wine:
The seas could not insapphirine the perfect azure of his
eyes.

His thick soft throat was white as milk and threaded
with thin veins of blue:
And curious pearls like frozen dew were broidered on
his flowing silk.

*

On pearl and porphyry pedestalled he was too bright to
look upon:
For on his ivory breast there shone the wondrous
ocean-emerald,

That mystic moonlit jewel which some diver of the
Colchian caves
Had found beneath the blackening waves and carried to
the Colchian witch.

Before his gilded galiot ran naked vine-wreathed
    Corybants,
And lines of swaying elephants knelt down to draw his
    chariot,

And lines of swarthy Nubians bare up his litter as he
    rode
Down the great granite-paven road between the
    nodding peacock-fans.

The merchants brought him steatite from Sidon in their
    painted ships:
The meanest cup that touched his lips was fashioned
    from a chrysolite.

The merchants brought him cedar-chests of rich apparel
    bound with cords:
His train was borne by Memphian Lords: young Kings
    were glad to be his guests.

Ten hundred shaven priests did bow to Ammon's altar
    day and night,
Ten hundred lamps did wave their light through
    Ammon's carven house – and now

Foul snake and speckled adder with their young ones
    crawl from stone to stone
For ruined is the house and prone the great rose-
    marble monolith!

Wild ass or trotting jackal comes and couches in the
    mouldering gates:
Wild satyrs call unto their mates across the fallen fluted
    drums.

And on the summit of the pile the blue-faced ape of
    Horus sits

And gibbers while the figtree splits the pillars of the
    peristyle.

*

The god is scattered here and there: deep hidden in the
    windy sand
I saw his giant granite hand still clenched in impotent
    despair.

And many a wandering caravan of stately negroes
    silken-shawled,
Crossing the desert, halts appalled before the neck that
    none can span.

And many a bearded Bedouin draws back his yellow-
    striped burnous
To gaze upon the Titan thews of him who was thy
    paladin.

*

Go, seek his fragments on the moor and wash them in
    the evening dew,
And from their pieces make anew thy mutilated
    paramour!

Go, seek them where they lie alone and from their
    broken pieces make
Thy bruisèd bedfellow! and wake mad passions in the
    senseless stone!

Charm his dull ear with Syrian hymns! He loved your
    body! Oh, be kind,
Pour spikenard on his hair, and wind soft rolls of linen
    round his limbs!

Wind round his head the figured coins! Stain with red
fruits those pallid lips!
Weave purple for his shrunken hips! and purple for his
barren loins!

*

Away to Egypt! Have no fear. Only one God has ever
died.
Only one God has let his side be wounded by a
soldier's spear.

But these, thy lovers, are not dead. Still by the
hundred-cubit gate
Dog-faced Anubis sits in state with lotus-lilies for thy
head.

Still from his chair of porphyry gaunt Memnon strains
his lidless eyes
Across the empty land, and cries each yellow morning
unto thee.

And Nilus with his broken horn lies in his black and
oozy bed
And till thy coming will not spread his waters on the
withering corn.

Your lovers are not dead, I know. They will rise up
and hear your voice
And clash their cymbals and rejoice and run to kiss
your mouth! And so,

Set wings upon your argosies! Set horses to your ebon
car!
Back to your Nile! Or if you are grown sick of dead
divinities

Follow some roving lion's spoor across the copper-
coloured plain,
Reach out and hale him by the mane and bid him be
your paramour!

Couch by his side upon the grass and set your white
teeth in his throat
And when you hear his dying note lash your long
flanks of polished brass

And take a tiger for your mate, whose amber sides are
flecked with black,
And ride upon his gilded back in triumph through the
Theban gate,

And toy with him in amorous jests, and when he
turns, and snarls, and gnaws,
O smite him with your jasper claws! and bruise him
with your agate breasts!

*

Why are you tarrying? Get hence! I weary of your
sullen ways,
I weary of your steadfast gaze, your somnolent
magnificence.

Your horrible and heavy breath makes the light flicker
in the lamp,
And on my brow I feel the damp and dreadful dews of
night and death.

Your eyes are like fantastic moons that shiver in some
stagnant lake,
Your tongue is like a scarlet snake that dances to
fantastic tunes,

Your pulse makes poisonous melodies, and your black
    throat is like the hole
Left by some torch or burning coal on Saracenic
    tapestries.

Away! the sulphur-coloured stars are hurrying through
    the Western Gate!
Away! or it may be too late to climb their silent silver
    cars!

See, the dawn shivers round the grey gilt-dialled
    towers, and the rain
Streams down each diamonded pane and blurs with
    tears the wannish day.

What snake-tressed Fury fresh from Hell, with uncouth
    gestures and unclean,
Stole from the poppy-drowsy Queen and led you to a
    student's cell?

                *

What songless tongueless Ghost of Sin crept through
    the curtains of the night,
And saw my taper burning bright, and knocked, and
    bade you enter in.

Are there not others more accursed, whiter with
    leprosies than I?
Are Abana and Pharphar dry that you come here to
    slake your thirst?

Get hence, you loathsome Mystery! Hideous animal, get
    hence!
You wake in me each bestial sense, you make me what
    I would not be.

You make my creed a barren sham, you wake foul
dreams of sensual life,
And Atys with his blood-stained knife were better than
the thing I am.

False Sphinx! False Sphinx! by reedy Styx old Charon,
leaning on his oar,
Waits for my coin. Go thou before, and leave me to
my Crucifix,

Whose pallid burden, sick with pain, watches the
world with wearied eyes,
And weeps for every soul that dies, and weeps for
every soul in vain.

In Memoriam
C. T. W.
Sometime Trooper of the Royal Horse Guards.
Obiit H.M. Prison, Reading, Berkshire,
July 7th, 1896.

The Ballad of Reading Gaol By C.3.3.

I

He did not wear his scarlet coat,
  For blood and wine are red,
And blood and wine were on his hands
  When they found him with the dead,
The poor dead woman whom he loved,
  And murdered in her bed.

He walked amongst the Trial Men
  In a suit of shabby gray;
A cricket cap was on his head,
  And his step seemed light and gay;
But I never saw a man who looked
  So wistfully at the day.

I never saw a man who looked
  With such a wistful eye
Upon that little tent of blue
  Which prisoners call the sky,
And at every drifting cloud that went
  With sails of silver by.

I walked, with other souls in pain,
  Within another ring,

And was wondering if the man had done
  A great or little thing,
When a voice behind me whispered low,
  'That fellow's got to swing.'

Dear Christ! the very prison walls
  Suddenly seemed to reel,
And the sky above my head became
  Like a casque of scorching steel;
And, though I was a soul in pain,
  My pain I could not feel.

I only knew what hunted thought
  Quickened his step, and why
He looked upon the garish day
  With such a wistful eye;
The man had killed the thing he loved,
  And so he had to die.

          *

Yet each man kills the thing he loves,
  By each let this be heard,
Some do it with a bitter look,
  Some with a flattering word,
The coward does it with a kiss,
  The brave man with a sword!

Some kill their love when they are young,
  And some when they are old;
Some strangle with the hands of Lust,
  Some with the hands of Gold:
The kindest use a knife, because
  The dead so soon grow cold.

Some love too little, some too long,
  Some sell, and others buy;
Some do the deed with many tears,
  And some without a sigh:
For each man kills the thing he loves,
  Yet each man does not die.

*

He does not die a death of shame
  On a day of dark disgrace,
Nor have a noose about his neck,
  Nor a cloth upon his face,
Nor drop feet foremost through the floor
  Into an empty space.

He does not sit with silent men
  Who watch him night and day;
Who watch him when he tries to weep,
  And when he tries to pray;
Who watch him lest himself should rob
  The prison of its prey.

He does not wake at dawn to see
  Dread figures throng his room,
The shivering Chaplain robed in white,
  The Sheriff stern with gloom,
And the Governor all in shiny black,
  With the yellow face of Doom.

He does not rise in piteous haste
  To put on convict-clothes,
While some coarse-mouthed Doctor gloats, and notes

Each new and nerve-twitched pose,
Fingering a watch whose little ticks
  Are like horrible hammer-blows.

He does not know that sickening thirst
  That sands one's throat, before
The hangman with his gardener's gloves
  Slips through the padded door,
And binds one with three leathern thongs,
  That the throat may thirst no more.

He does not bend his head to hear
  The Burial Office read,
Nor, while the terror of his soul
  Tells him he is not dead,
Cross his own coffin, as he moves
  Into the hideous shed.

He does not stare upon the air
  Through a little roof of glass:
He does not pray with lips of clay
  For his agony to pass;
Nor feel upon his shuddering cheek
  The kiss of Caiaphas.

II

Six weeks our guardsman walked the yard,
  In the suit of shabby gray:
His cricket cap was on his head,
  And his step seemed light and gay,
But I never saw a man who looked
  So wistfully at the day.

I never saw a man who looked
  With such a wistful eye
Upon that little tent of blue
  Which prisoners call the sky,
And at every wandering cloud that trailed
  Its ravelled fleeces by.

He did not wring his hands, as do
  Those witless men who dare
To try to rear the changeling Hope
  In the cave of black Despair:
He only looked upon the sun,
  And drank the morning air.

He did not wring his hands nor weep,
  Nor did he peek or pine,
But he drank the air as though it held
  Some healthful anodyne;
With open mouth he drank the sun
  As though it had been wine!

And I and all the souls in pain,
  Who tramped the other ring,
Forgot if we ourselves had done
  A great or little thing,
And watched with gaze of dull amaze
  The man who had to swing.

And strange it was to see him pass
  With a step so light and gay,
And strange it was to see him look
  So wistfully at the day,
And strange it was to think that he
  Had such a debt to pay.

For oak and elm have pleasant leaves
  That in the spring-time shoot:
But grim to see is the gallows-tree,
  With its adder-bitten root,
And, green or dry, a man must die
  Before it bears its fruit!

The loftiest place is that seat of grace
  For which all wordlings try:
But who would stand in hempen band
  Upon a scaffold high,
And through a murderer's collar take
  His last look at the sky?

It is sweet to dance to violins
  When Love and Life are fair:
To dance to flutes, to dance to lutes
  Is delicate and rare:
But it is not sweet with nimble feet
  To dance upon the air!

So with curious eyes and sick surmise
  We watched him day by day,
And wondered if each one of us
  Would end the self-same way,
For none can tell to what red Hell
  His sightless soul may stray.

*

At last the dead man walked no more
  Amongst the Trial Men,
And I knew that he was standing up

94

In the black dock's dreadful pen,
And that never would I see his face
  In God's sweet world again.

Like two doomed ships that pass in storm
  We had crossed each other's way:
But we made no sign, we said no word,
  We had no word to say;
For we did not meet in the holy night,
  But in the shameful day.

A prison wall was round us both,
  Two outcast men we were:
The world had thrust us from its heart,
  And God from out His care:
And the iron gin that waits for Sin
  Had caught us in its snare.

III

In Debtors' Yard the stones are hard,
  And the dripping wall is high,
So it was there he took the air
  Beneath the leaden sky,
And by each side a Warder walked,
  For fear the man might die.

Or else he sat with those who watched
  His anguish night and day;
Who watched him when he rose to weep,
  And when he crouched to pray;
Who watched him lest himself should rob
  Their scaffold of its prey.

The Governor was strong upon
  The Regulations Act:
The Doctor said that Death was but
  A scientific fact:
And twice a day the Chaplain called,
  And left a little tract.

And twice a day he smoked his pipe,
  And drank his quart of beer:
His soul was resolute, and held
  No hiding-place for fear;
He often said that he was glad
  The hangman's hands were near.

But why he said so strange a thing
  No Warder dared to ask:
For he to whom a watcher's doom
  Is given as his task,
Must set a lock upon his lips,
  And make his face a mask.

Or else he might be moved, and try
  To comfort or console:
And what should Human Pity do
  Pent up in Murderers' Hole?
What word of grace in such a place
  Could help a brother's soul?

*

With slouch and swing around the ring
  We trod the Fools' Parade!
We did not care: we knew we were

The Devil's Own Brigade:
And shaven head and feet of lead
  Make a merry masquerade.

We tore the tarry rope to shreds
  With blunt and bleeding nails;
We rubbed the doors, and scrubbed the floors,
  And cleaned the shining rails:
And, rank by rank, we soaped the plank,
  And clattered with the pails.

We sewed the sacks, we broke the stones,
  We turned the dusty drill:
We banged the tins, and bawled the hymns,
  And sweated on the mill:
But in the heart of every man
  Terror was lying still.

So still it lay that every day
  Crawled like a weed-clogged wave:
And we forgot the bitter lot
  That waits for fool and knave,
Till once, as we tramped in from work,
  We passed an open grave.

With yawning mouth the yellow hole
  Gaped for a living thing;
The very mud cried out for blood
  To the thirsty asphalte ring:
And we knew that ere one dawn grew fair
  Some prisoner had to swing.

Right in we went, with soul intent
  On Death and Dread and Doom:
The hangman, with his little bag,

Went shuffling through the gloom:
And each man trembled as he crept
    Into his numbered tomb.

            *

That night the empty corridors
    Were full of forms of Fear,
And up and down the iron town
    Stole feet we could not hear,
And through the bars that hide the stars
    White faces seemed to peer.

He lay as one who lies and dreams
    In a pleasant meadow-land,
The watchers watched him as he slept,
    And could not understand
How one could sleep so sweet a sleep
    With a hangman close at hand.

But there is no sleep when men must weep
    Who never yet have wept:
So we – the fool, the fraud, the knave—
    That endless vigil kept,
And through each brain on hands of pain
    Another's terror crept.

            *

Alas! it is a fearful thing
    To feel another's guilt!
For, right within, the sword of Sin
    Pierced to its poisoned hilt,
And as molten lead were the tears we shed
    For the blood we had not spilt.

The Warders with their shoes of felt
  Crept by each padlocked door,
And peeped and saw, with eyes of awe,
  Gray figures on the floor,
And wondered why men knelt to pray
  Who never prayed before.

All through the night we knelt and prayed,
  Mad mourners of a corse!
The troubled plumes of midnight were
  The plumes upon a hearse:
And bitter wine upon a sponge
  Was the savour of Remorse.

*

The gray cock crew, the red cock crew,
  But never came the day:
And crooked shapes of Terror crouched,
  In the corners where we lay:
And each evil sprite that walks by night
  Before us seemed to play.

They glided past, they glided fast,
  Like travellers through a mist:
They mocked the moon in a rigadoon
  Of delicate turn and twist,
And with formal pace and loathsome grace
  The phantoms kept their tryst.

With mop and mow, we saw them go,
  Slim shadows hand in hand:
About, about, in ghostly rout

They trod a saraband:
And the damned grotesques made arabesques,
  Like the wind upon the sand!

With pirouettes of marionettes,
  They tripped on pointed tread:
But with flutes of Fear they filled the ear,
  As their grisly masque they led,
And loud they sang, and long they sang,
  For they sang to wake the dead.

'Oho!' they cried, *'The world is wide,*
  But fettered limbs go lame!
And once, or twice, to throw the dice
  Is a gentlemanly game,
But he does not win who plays with Sin
  In the secret House of Shame.'

                    *

No things of air these antics were,
  That frolicked with such glee:
To men whose lives were held in gyves,
  And whose feet might not go free,
Ah! wounds of Christ! they were living things,
  Most terrible to see.

Around, around, they waltzed and wound;
  Some wheeled in smirking pairs;
With the mincing step of a demirep
  Some sidled up the stairs:
And with subtle sneer, and fawning leer,
  Each helped us at our prayers.

The morning wind began to moan,
  But still the night went on:
Through its giant loom the web of gloom
  Crept till each thread was spun:
And, as we prayed, we grew afraid
  Of the Justice of the Sun.

The moaning wind went wandering round
  The weeping prison-wall:
Till like a wheel of turning steel
  We felt the minutes crawl:
O moaning wind! what had we done
  To have such a seneschal?

At last I saw the shadowed bars,
  Like a lattice wrought in lead,
Move right across the whitewashed wall
  That faced my three-plank bed,
And I knew that somewhere in the world
  God's dreadful dawn was red.

*

At six o'clock we cleaned our cells,
  At seven all was still,
But the sough and swing of a mighty wing
  The prison seemed to fill,
For the Lord of Death with icy breath
  Had entered in to kill.

He did not pass in purple pomp,
  Nor ride a moon-white steed.
Three yards of cord and a standing board

Are all the gallows' need:
So with rope of shame the Herald came
    To do the secret deed.

    *

We were as men who through a fen
    Of filthy darkness grope:
We did not dare to breathe a prayer,
    Or to give our anguish scope:
Something was dead in each of us,
    And what was dead was Hope.

For Man's grim Justice goes its way,
    And will not swerve aside:
It slays the weak, it slays the strong,
    It has a deadly stride:
With iron heel it slays the strong,
    The monstrous parricide!

    *

We waited for the stroke of eight:
    Each tongue was thick with thirst:
For the stroke of eight is the stroke of Fate
    That makes a man accursed,
And Fate will use a running noose
    For the best man and the worst.

We had no other thing to do,
    Save to wait for the sign to come:
So, like things of stone in a valley lone,
    Quiet we sat and dumb:
But each man's heart beat thick and quick,
    Like a madman on a drum!

With sudden shock the prison-clock
  Smote on the shivering air,
And from all the gaol rose up a wail
  Of impotent despair,
Like the sound that frightened marshes hear
  From some leper in his lair.

And as one sees most fearful things
  In the crystal of a dream,
We saw the greasy hempen rope
  Hooked to the blackened beam,
And heard the prayer the hangman's snare
  Strangled into a scream.

And all the woe that moved him so
  That he gave that bitter cry,
And the wild regrets, and bloody sweats,
  None knew so well as I:
For he who lives more lives than one
  More deaths than one must die.

IV

There is no chapel on the day
  On which they hang a man:
The Chaplain's heart is far too sick,
  Or his face is far too wan,
Or there is that written in his eyes
  Which none should look upon.

So they kept us close till nigh on noon,
  And then they rang the bell,
And the Warders with their jingling keys
  Opened each listening cell,
And down the iron stair we tramped,
  Each from his separate Hell.

Out into God's sweet air we went,
  But not in wonted way,
For this man's face was white with fear,
  And that man's face was gray,
And I never saw sad men who looked
  So wistfully at the day.

I never saw sad men who looked
  With such a wistful eye
Upon the little tent of blue
  We prisoners called the sky,
And at every careless cloud that passed
  In happy freedom by.

But there were those amongst us all
  Who walked with downcast head,
And knew that, had each got his due,
  They should have died instead:
He had but killed a thing that lived,
  Whilst they had killed the dead.

For he who sins a second time
  Wakes a dead soul to pain,
And draws it from its spotted shroud,
  And makes it bleed again,
And makes it bleed great gouts of blood,
  And makes it bleed in vain!

Like ape or clown, in monstrous garb
  With crooked arrows starred,
Silently we went round and round
  The slippery asphalte yard;
Silently we went round and round,
  And no man spoke a word.

Silently we went round and round,
  And through each hollow mind
The Memory of dreadful things
  Rushed like a dreadful wind,
And Horror stalked before each man,
  And Terror crept behind.

*

The Warders strutted up and down,
  And kept their herd of brutes,
Their uniforms were spick and span,
  And they wore their Sunday suits,
But we knew the work they had been at,
  By the quicklime on their boots.

For where a grave had opened wide,
  There was no grave at all:
Only a stretch of mud and sand
  By the hideous prison-wall,
And a little heap of burning lime,
  That the man should have his pall.

For he has a pall, this wretched man,
  Such as few can claim:
Deep down below a prison-yard,

Naked for greater shame,
He lies, with fetters on each foot,
  Wrapt in a sheet of flame!

And all the while the burning lime
  Eats flesh and bone away,
It eats the brittle bone by night,
  And the soft flesh by day,
It eats the flesh and bone by turns,
  But it eats the heart alway.

       *

For three long years they will not sow
  Or root or seedling there:
For three long years the unblessed spot
  Will sterile be and bare,
And look upon the wondering sky
  With unreproachful stare.

They think a murderer's heart would taint
  Each simple seed they sow.
It is not true! God's kindly earth
  Is kindlier than men know,
And the red rose would but blow more red,
  The white rose whiter blow.

Out of his mouth a red, red rose!
  Out of his heart a white!
For who can say by what strange way,
  Christ brings His will to light,
Since the barren staff the pilgrim bore
  Bloomed in the great Pope's sight?

But neither milk-white rose nor red
  May bloom in prison air;
The shard, the pebble, and the flint,
  Are what they give us there:
For flowers have been known to heal
  A common man's despair.

So never will wine-red rose or white,
  Petal by petal, fall
On that stretch of mud and sand that lies
  By the hideous prison-wall,
To tell the men who tramp the yard
  That God's Son died for all.

*

Yet though the hideous prison-wall
  Still hems him round and round,
And a spirit may not walk by night
  That is with fetters bound,
And a spirit may but weep that lies
  In such unholy ground,

He is at peace – this wretched man—
  At peace, or will be soon:
There is no thing to make him mad,
  Nor does Terror walk at noon,
For the lampless Earth in which he lies
  Has neither Sun nor Moon.

*

They hanged him as a beast is hanged:
  They did not even toll
A requiem that might have brought
  Rest to his startled soul,
But hurriedly they took him out,
  And hid him in a hole.

They stripped him of his canvas clothes,
  And gave him to the flies:
They mocked the swollen purple throat,
  And the stark and staring eyes:
And with laughter loud they heaped the shroud
  In which their convict lies.

The Chaplain would not kneel to pray
  By his dishonoured grave:
Nor mark it with that blessed Cross
  That Christ for sinners gave,
Because the man was one of those
  Whom Christ came down to save.

Yet all is well; he has but passed
  To Life's appointed bourne:
And alien tears will fill for him
  Pity's long-broken urn,
For his mourners will be outcast men,
  And outcasts always mourn.

V

I know not whether Laws be right,
  Or whether Laws be wrong;
All that we know who lie in gaol

Is that the wall is strong;
And that each day is like a year,
  A year whose days are long.

But this I know, that every Law
  That men have made for Man,
Since first Man took his brother's life,
  And the sad world began,
But straws the wheat and saves the chaff
  With a most evil fan.

This too I know — and wise it were
  If each could know the same—
That every prison that men build
  Is built with bricks of shame,
And bound with bars lest Christ should see
  How men their brothers maim.

With bars they blur the gracious moon,
  And blind the goodly sun:
And they do well to hide their Hell,
  For in it things are done
That Son of God nor son of Man
  Ever should look upon!

*

The vilest deeds like poison weeds
  Bloom well in prison-air:
It is only what is good in Man
  That wastes and withers there:
Pale Anguish keeps the heavy gate,
  And the Warder is Despair.

For they starve the little frightened child
  Till it weeps both night and day:
And they scourge the weak, and flog the fool,
  And gibe the old and gray,
And some grow mad, and all grow bad,
  And none a word may say.

Each narrow cell in which we dwell
  Is a foul and dark latrine,
And fetid breath of living Death
  Chokes up each grated screen,
And all, but Lust, is turned to dust
  In Humanity's machine.

The brackish water that we drink
  Creeps with a loathsome slime,
And the bitter bread they weigh in scales
  Is full of chalk and lime,
And Sleep will not lie down, but walks
  Wild-eyed, and cries to Time.

*

But though lean Hunger and green Thirst
  Like asp with adder fight,
We have little care of prison fare,
  For what chills and kills outright
Is that every stone one lifts by day
  Becomes one's heart by night.

With midnight always in one's heart,
  And twilight in one's cell,
We turn the crank, or tear the rope,

Each in his separate Hell,
And the silence is more awful far
  Than the sound of a brazen bell.

And never a human voice comes near
  To speak a gentle word:
And the eye that watches through the door
  Is pitiless and hard:
And by all forgot, we rot and rot,
  With soul and body marred.

And thus we rust Life's iron chain
  Degraded and alone:
And some men curse, and some men weep,
  And some men make no moan:
But God's eternal Laws are kind
  And break the heart of stone.

                *

And every human heart that breaks,
  In prison-cell or yard,
Is as that broken box that gave
  Its treasure to the Lord,
And filled the unclean leper's house
  With the scent of costliest nard.

Ah! happy they whose hearts can break
  And peace of pardon win!
How else may man make straight his plan
  And cleanse his soul from Sin?
How else but through a broken heart
  May Lord Christ enter in?

                *

And he of the swollen purple throat,
  And the stark and staring eyes,
Waits for the holy hands that took
  The Thief to Paradise;
And a broken and a contrite heart
  The Lord will not despise.

The man in red who reads the Law
  Gave him three weeks of life,
Three little weeks in which to heal
  His soul of his soul's strife,
And cleanse from every blot of blood
  The hand that held the knife.

And with tears of blood he cleansed the hand,
  The hand that held the steel:
For only blood can wipe out blood,
  And only tears can heal:
And the crimson stain that was of Cain
  Became Christ's snow-white seal.

VI

In Reading gaol by Reading town
  There is a pit of shame,
And in it lies a wretched man
  Eaten by teeth of flame,
In a burning winding-sheet he lies,
  And his grave has got no name.

And there, till Christ call forth the dead,
  In silence let him lie:
No need to waste the foolish tear,

Or heave the windy sigh:
The man had killed the thing he loved,
  And so he had to die.

And all men kill the thing they love,
  By all let this be heard,
Some do it with a bitter look,
  Some with a flattering word,
The coward does it with a kiss,
  The brave man with a sword!

                                    C.3.3

Glossary of Classical Allusions

ACTÆON, a hunter who accidentally spied on the goddess Artemis while she bathed. As a punishment he was transformed into a stag, and torn apart by his own hounds.

ADONIS, a beautiful youth who, in one tradition, is wooed by Aphrodite.

APHRODITE, the Greek goddess of love, called Venus in Roman myths.

ARCADY or ARCADIA, a region of Greece, the importance of which is more symbolic and poetical than geographical or historical. In poetry, the region has come to denote an ideal realm of pastoral simplicity, and has associations with the 'Golden Age'.

ARTEMIS, Greek goddess of the hunt, and traditionally depicted as a virgin.

ATHENA, Greek goddess who was also patron of Athens, the city which bore her name.

DIANA, the Roman equivalent of Artemis.

DIONYSUS, Greek god of wine and ecstasy. His worship is associated with revelry, riot and even madness.

EROS, the god of love, called Cupid by the Romans.

ENDYMION, a beautiful youth who was loved by the moon. He was put into a perpetual sleep, and every night the moon (Cynthia or Diana) embraced him. The title of a poem by John Keats who treated this theme.

HERACLES, called Hercules in Roman mythology, he was famous for his strength and his feats of bravery.

HYACINTH, a beautiful youth beloved of Apollo, accidentally killed by the god when his discus struck him.

NARCISSUS, a beautiful youth who spurned all suitors, and fell in love with his own reflection in a pool.

PAN, in Greek mythology he is the god of flocks and shepherds, and associated with Arcadia. He is renowned for his musical ability.

PERSEPHONE or PROSERPINE, Persephone is the name given by the Greeks to the queen of the Underworld (Proserpine is the Roman name). A goddess who was daughter of Zeus and Demeter (the corn goddess), she was carried off by Hades and forced to spend six months of each year with him in the Underworld.

SATYRS, woodland demi-gods, who were half men and half goats. Renowned for their lewdness and drunken revelry. Often attendants to Dionysus.

Chronology of Wilde's Life

Year	Age	Life
1854		Born in Dublin 16 October
1864–71	10–17	Attends Portora Royal School, Enniskillen
1871–4	17–20	Reading Classics at Trinity College, Dublin. Granted scholarship to Magdalen College, Oxford
1874–8	20–24	Takes First in Classical Moderations (1876) and in Literae Humaniores (1878). Wins the Newdigate Prize for Poetry with 'Ravenna'
1879	25	Moves to London, as self-styled 'professor of aesthetics'
1881	27	Poems published
1884	30	Marries Constance Lloyd; moves to Chelsea. Begins regular book-reviewing
1885	31	Son Cyril born
1886	32	Son Vyvyan born. Wilde meets Robert Ross
1888	34	The Happy Prince and Other Tales published
1890	36	First version of The Picture of Dorian Gray published

Chronology of his Times

Year	Artistic Events	Historical Events
1854–6		Crimean War
1856	Flaubert, Madame Bovary	
1857	Baudelaire, Les fleurs du mal	Indian rising ('Mutiny')
1864	Browning, Dramatis Personae Newman, Apologia pro Vita Sua	
1871	Eliot, Middlemarch Swinburne, Songs before Sunrise	Trade Unions legalised Paris Commune
1874	Flaubert, Temptation of St Antony Monet's 'Impression: Sunrise' exhibited Eliot, Daniel Deronda	Disraeli becomes Prime Minister
1879	Meredith, The Egoist Ibsen, A Doll's House	London telephone exchange established
1880	Death of George Eliot	Gladstone becomes (Liberal) Prime Minister
1881	James, The Portrait of a Lady D. G. Rossetti, Ballads and Sonnets Gilbert and Sullivan's Patience is produced	Irish Land Law Act
1884	J-K Huysmans, A Rebours	The Mahdi takes Omdurman
1885	Pater, Marius the Epicurean Whistler delivers his 'Ten O'Clock Lecture'	Berlin Conference Gordon dies at Khartoum Criminal Law Amendment Act (against homosexual practices)
1886	R. L. Stevenson, Dr Jekyll and Mr Hyde Krafft-Ebbing, Psychopathia Sexualis	Gladstone re-elected Irish Home Rule Bill defeated
1888	Arnold, Essays in Criticism (second series)	Local Government Act Eastman's Kodak box camera
1890	Ibsen, Hedda Gabler James, The Tragic Muse Death of Newman	Parnell resigns as Irish Nationalist leader

Year	Age	Life
1891	37	*The Duchess of Padua* — with the title *Guido Ferranti* — produced in New York. Meets Lord Alfred Douglas. Publishes the revised *Dorian Gray*, *Intentions*, *Lord Arthur Savile's Crime and Other Stories* and *A House of Pomegranates*.
1892	38	*Lady Windermere's Fan* produced. London production of *Salomé* refused theatre licence.
1893	39	*Salomé* published in English translation. *The Sphinx* and *A Woman of No Importance* published
1895	41	*An Ideal Husband* and *The Importance of Being Earnest* produced. Wilde unsuccessfully sues the Marquess of Queensbury for criminal libel. Wilde charged with 'acts of gross indecency with other male persons' and given two years hard labour, served at Holloway, Pentonville, Wandsworth and Reading Gaol
1896	42	Death of mother. *Salomé* produced in Paris
1897	43	Writes *De Profundis* in prison. On release settles at Bernevale, near Dieppe, then visits Italy with Douglas
1898	44	*The Ballad of Reading Gaol* published. Moves to Paris. Death of Constance Wilde
1900	46	Visits Rome and Naples. Returns to Paris. Baptized a Roman Catholic during severe illness. Dies 30 November

Year	Artistic Events	Historical Events
1891	Hardy, *Tess of the D'Urbevilles* Morris, *News from Nowhere*	
1892	Kipling, *Barrack Room Ballads* Death of Whitman Death of Tennyson	Gladstone's fourth Ministry
1893	Pater, *Plato and Platonism*	Independent Labour Party formed Lords reject Irish Home Rule Bill
1895	Hardy, *Jude the Obscure* Pater, *Greek Studies* Yeats, *Poems* Max Nordau's *Degeneration* (1893) translated into English	Lumière Brothers invent cinematography Jameson Raid into the Transvaal
1896	A. E. Houseman, *A Shropshire Lad*	
1897	James, *What Maisie Knew* Havelock Ellis, *Sexual Inversion*	Queen Victoria's Diamond Jubilee Second Colonial Conference
1898	Hardy, *Wessex Poems* James, *The Turn of the Screw*	Kitchener defeats Dervishes at Omdurman
1900	Conrad, *Lord Jim* Shaw, *Three Plays for Puritans* Death of Ruskin	British Labour Party founded Relief of Ladysmith and Mafeking

Acknowledgements

I would like to thank the following institutions for their help in preparing this edition, and for allowing me to make use of manuscripts. The Master and Fellows of University College, Oxford; The William Andrews Clark Memorial Library; University of California, Los Angeles; The British Library; The Bodleian Library, Oxford. I would especially like to acknowledge my gratitude to the Estate of Oscar Wilde, represented with great warmth and scholarly acumen by his grandson Merlin Holland.